IF
YOU
SNOOZE
You Might Miss a Moose

written by
Patricia Dickison Elliott

IF YOU SNOOZE
You Might Miss a Moose
2018 Copyright by Patricia Dickison Elliott
All Rights Reserved

Published by Kids Book Press
An imprint of A & S Publishing, A & S Holmes, inc.
Sharon Kizziah-Holmes – Publishing Coordinator

ISBN: 978-1-945669-46-0

DEDICATION

For Olivia and Nathan, of course.

ACKNOWLEDGMENTS

Thank you to the Harris family for making our trip to Yellowstone possible.
Thanks to Aleta Harris for taking and sharing some of the photos in this book.

Hi, I'm Nathan. My family went to Yellowstone National Park on a vacation. I was really excited.

We planned things we wanted to see. I made a list of the animals and a map of the waterfalls and geysers.

You wouldn't believe my sister. Her name is Olivia. She slept so much she nearly missed seeing Yellowstone Park.

I'm not joking. That girl slept through most of our vacation.

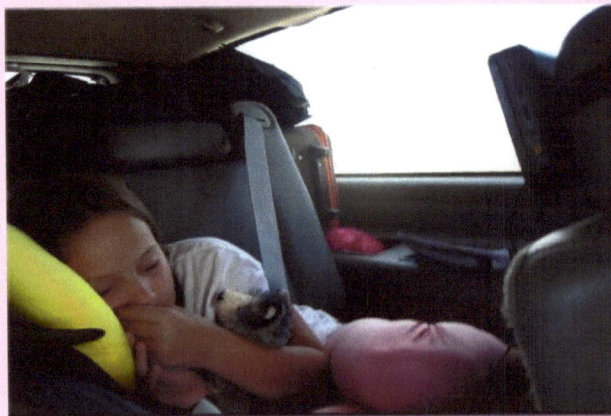

There was a big herd of bison, some people call them buffalo.

They stood in the road and we couldn't pass.

. Mom and I snapped picture after picture, and there was Olivia sound asleep in the back seat of the car.

z z z
z
z z
z z z z z z

This is the paint pots. Whew they stink. The colors are awesome though, and they make a plop plop noise.

We were warned not to get too near them. Because the ground was so soft and unsafe, we were told not to walk anywhere but on the walkway.

My grandma's cap flew off and landed just outside the walkway. Dad had to reach a long way to get it to stay safe on the walkway. But Olivia, my sleeping sister, didn't see any of that.

We found a picnic table under a shady tree in Mammoth.

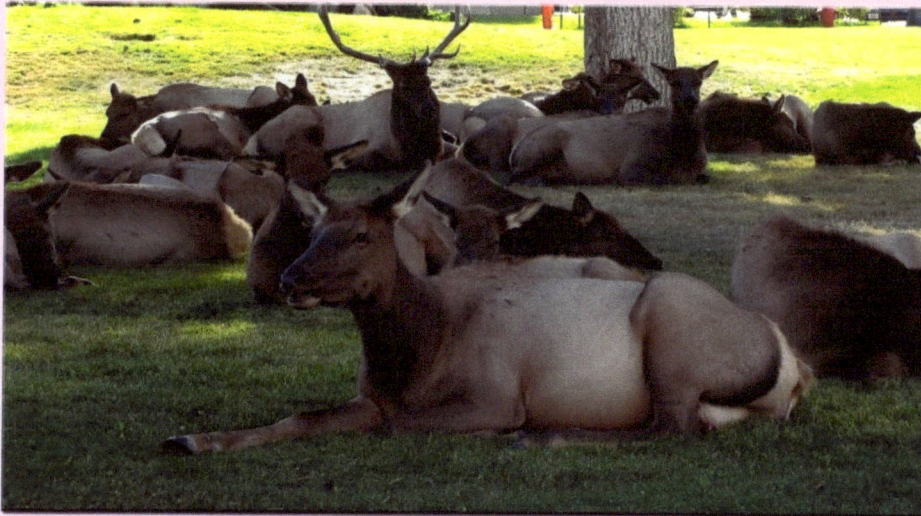

There were elk just walking around or lying on the lawn. That was cool. Olivia missed all that, too. She was z^z asleep.

When Olivia woke up she wanted to know when we were having lunch. We just laughed at her and told her she missed lunch. We told her about the bison herd and the elk.

When she realized all she missed, she decided to stay awake.

We stopped at Fire in the Hole and had a swim. That was a bit chilly but at least we could say we swam in the Yellowstone River.

Olivia got excited when she saw the waterfalls. The river runs swiftly down and pours over rocks into a pool below.

She thought they were pretty. I guess they were but I liked looking for more animals. We had binoculars and searched in the fields.

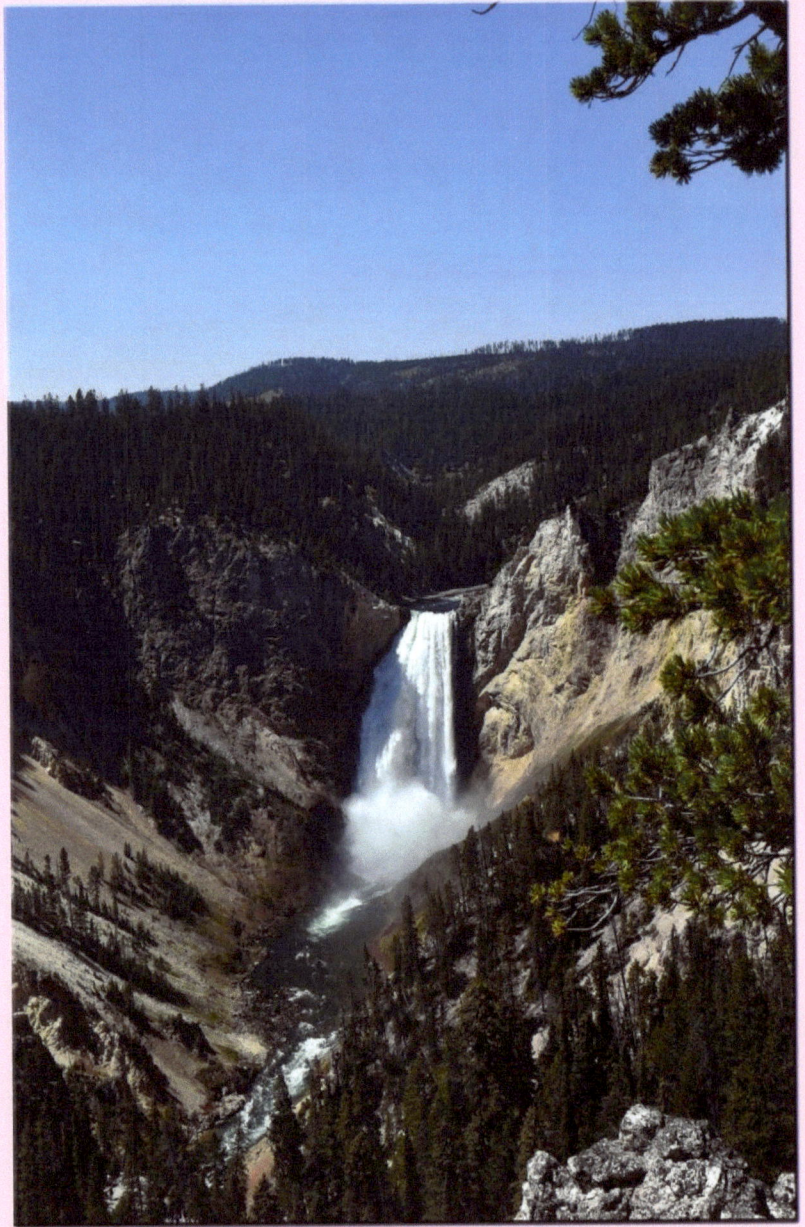

Oh look. Mom is watching something in the hills. She has the binoculars.

Where are my binoculars? Are you awake Olivia? There are two bears up on the hillside.

We all took a turn watching them. A lot of people stopped their cars to watch the bears play.

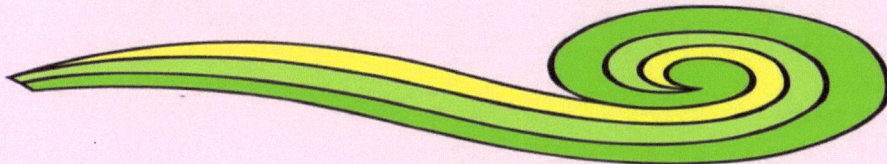

Old Faithful geyser is something else. It is awesome. I couldn't believe how high it went. There are several geysers in Yellowstone but Old Faithful is the biggest.

Don't go to sleep Olivia. We will have dinner at the lodge, then we are going to sit out and watch for animals as it gets dark.

They come out to feed right before they go to bed. Stay awake Olivia. This will be fun.

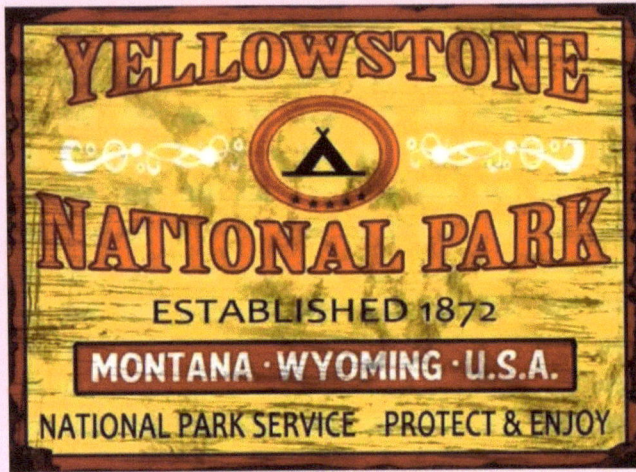
YELLOWSTONE
NATIONAL PARK
ESTABLISHED 1872
MONTANA · WYOMING · U.S.A.
NATIONAL PARK SERVICE   PROTECT & ENJOY

Old Faithful Lodge

Then

Now

Did you know this place was established as a
National Park almost 150 years ago?

Olivia has some advice for people visiting the National Parks. "Don't go to sleep or you will miss something exciting like a moose or a beaver or a geyser spouting up.

The End...'Til Next Time

ABOUT THE AUTHOR

Pat lives and writes in the beautiful Missouri Ozarks. Her publication credits include Bible studies, articles, short stories and the first novel in the Lacy James Mysteries 'Murder on Tour'. She is a genealogist and has traced her family back to Germany and England. She photographs every old building and mill she sees and the family is sure the only pictures she takes while traveling are cemeteries. She loves to travel and often writes about her travels. Those settings and experiences usually end up in her stories.

Use the next few pages to write about YOUR favorite vacation. Draw
pictures of your family, animals or whatever you want.
Have a good time!

Have Fun

Have Fun

Have Fun

Have Fun

www.ingramcontent.com/pod-product-compliance
Lightning Source LLC
Chambersburg PA
CBHW040024050426

42452CB00002B/118